Cutting Edge Careers in
INFO TECH

Leanne Currie-McGhee

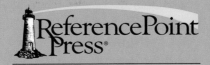

San Diego, CA

For more information, contact:
ReferencePoint Press, Inc.
PO Box 27779
San Diego, CA 92198
www.ReferencePointPress.com

Picture Credits:

Cover: puhhha/Shutterstock
 6: Maury Aaseng
12: GaudiLab/Shutterstock.com
27: Monstar Studio/Shutterstock.com
48: Gorodenkoff/Shutterstock.com
57: REDPIXEL.PR/Shutterstock.com
64: G-Stock Studio/Shutterstock.com

LIBRARY OF CONGRESS CATALOGING-IN-PUBLICATION DATA

Names: Currie-McGhee, L. K. (Leanne K.), author.
Title: Cutting edge careers in info tech / by Leanne Currie-McGhee.
Description: San Diego, CA : ReferencePoint Press, 2020. | Series: Cutting
   edge STEM careers | Includes bibliographical references and index.
Identifiers: LCCN 2019049384 (print) | LCCN 2019049385 (ebook) | ISBN
   9781682828694 (library binding) | ISBN 9781682828700 (ebook)
Subjects: LCSH: Information technology--Vocational guidance.
Classification: LCC T58.5 .C874 2020 (print) | LCC T58.5 (ebook) | DDC
   004.023--dc23
LC record available at https://lccn.loc.gov/2019049384
LC ebook record available at https://lccn.loc.gov/2019049385

Contents

Increasing Opportunities   4

Cloud Solutions Architect   8

Computer Vision Engineer   15

Cybersecurity Analyst   22

Data Scientist   30

Machine Learning Engineer   37

Mobile App Developer   44

User Interface Designer   52

Virtual Reality Developer   60

Source Notes   68
Interview with a Cloud Solutions Architect   72
Other Jobs in Information Technology   75
Index   76
About the Author   80

Increasing Opportunities

The information technology (IT) field is growing each day with increasing opportunities, particularly in areas where businesses and organizations are realizing how the technology can benefit their operations. Because of this, there is a growing need for people qualified in the latest areas of IT. Some IT jobs involve the use of computers to input, store, retrieve, and protect information. Others focus on networking computers or servers to speed the flow of information within companies, academic institutions, or other organizations. Still others involve designing software and user interfaces to bring applications and web pages to life. The IT field employs nearly 6 million individuals across a range of industries, including technology, health care, finance, and education. According to the Bureau of Labor Statistics, jobs in this industry are projected to be among the fastest growing in the nation, producing an 18 percent increase in the field through 2022.

Benefiting Businesses

While the IT industry overall is projected to grow, there are certain areas of IT that are predicted to experience more rapid growth than others. These include but are not limited to newer areas such as cloud computing, cybersecurity, big data, machine learning, vision engineering, and mobile applications. This is because businesses are discovering that if they harness the technology in these fields, they can improve their overall operations.

Cloud computing is expanding as both individuals and businesses find the benefits of uploading information from on-site computers to the internet and then accessing that information from any computer with web capabilities. *The cloud* is simply the term used to describe a network of remote servers that store data and are accessed via the internet. This allows organizations to reduce costs and network maintenance, since the hardware and software they use is not on-site but is instead maintained by their cloud service.

Big data is another major area of growth as companies and organizations take advantage of the latest methods of gathering and analyzing the immense amount of data available. Being able to navigate and utilize the data helps companies develop products tailored to customers. The field of big data, however, is not limited to commercial applications. For instance, structuring and interpreting data can help countries isolate health outbreaks or assist law enforcement. Bob Grove, chief operating officer of Edelman APAC, a global communications firm, explains that his company worked with the nonprofit group Stop the Traffik to gather and analyze data as part of an effort to combat human trafficking. The Edelman team of data and behavioral scientists focused on collecting and analyzing trafficking data to find clues. "The data allows us to identify trafficking hotspots and patterns, which are then shared with stakeholders that have been flagged as having links to trafficking-related activities," writes Grove. "For example, if our findings identify a particular airline route with a high rate of child trafficking victims, the airline can respond along that specific route right away."[1] Data scientists in this growing field are making impacts like this each day.

Like data science, cybersecurity is becoming a vital aspect of organizations and businesses. Cybersecurity professionals assess vulnerabilities and threats to an organization's hardware, software, programs, networks, and data and set up programs and firewalls to protect them. These professionals devise new programs to counter the increasing number of cyberattacks that threaten industry secrets, personal information, and even government elections. Equifax, an American credit reporting company, suffered a major cyberattack in 2017. The company's database of personal data (names, birth dates, Social Security numbers, and driver's license numbers) of 143 million American, Canadian, and British customers was breached. The theft nabbed roughly two hundred thousand credit card numbers as well. Incidents

Attributes That Matter to Employers

Written communication skills and the ability to solve problems are at the top of the list of attributes employers look for when considering new hires. This is the finding of a report titled "Job Outlook 2019." The report comes from the National Association of Colleges and Employers (NACE), an organization that surveys employers nationwide to learn more about their hiring plans in connection with recent college graduates. Other desirable attributes include the ability to work in a team setting, showing initiative, analytical skills, and a strong work ethic.

Attribute	% of Respondents
Communication skills (written)	82.0%
Problem-solving skills	80.9%
Ability to work in a team	78.7%
Initiative	74.2%
Analytical/quantitative skills	71.9%
Strong work ethic	70.8%
Communication skills (verbal)	67.4%
Leadership	67.4%
Detail oriented	59.6%
Technical skills	59.6%
Flexibility/adaptability	58.4%
Computer skills	55.1%
Interpersonal skills (relates well to others)	52.8%
Organizational ability	43.8%
Strategic planning skills	38.2%
Tactfulness	25.8%
Creativity	23.6%
Friendly/outgoing personality	22.5%
Entrepreneurial skills/risk-taker	16.9%
Fluency in a foreign language	11.2%

Source: "Job Outlook 2019," NACE, November 2018.
www.odu.edu/content/dam/odu/offices/cmc/docs/nace/2019-nace-job-outlook-survey.pdf.

like these threaten not just companies but utilities, transportation grids, and government infrastructure, making cybersecurity and other jobs in the IT industry vital. The IT information website eSecurity Planet noted in a 2019 survey that 57 percent of organizations plan to hire security staff in the coming year.

Fitting In to the Field

As cutting edge IT industries expand, more trained and talented professionals are in demand. The skill set for some jobs, such as data scientist and machine learning engineer, is acquired through extensive education. But for other positions, a passion and ability to learn quickly can get a talented individual far.

From cloud computing to virtual reality, innovative areas of IT are in need of individuals willing to learn fast. These fields are growing since companies and organizations see the possibilities of the advancing technologies and are in need of qualified people to implement these technologies. Those who love technology, embrace challenges, and work hard will experience fulfilling results.

Cloud Solutions Architect

What Does a Cloud Solutions Architect Do?

The cloud is a term for an internet-based information technology (IT) system where people and companies can store data and software applications. Data and applications are stored on servers that are located in many different places, hosted by another company, and accessed through wireless networks. In fact, most companies choose to store some or even the majority of their digital information and applications in the cloud for easy and safe access. Not maintaining their own storage servers also allows businesses to forgo the cost of housing, running, and maintaining these servers. Businesses that rely on cloud storage sometimes turn to a cloud solutions architect. This individual is the one who designs and oversees the implementation of cloud services for a company.

Cloud architects determine what servers will be used, where these servers are, and how they will be accessed. Their goal is to set up a cloud-hosting system that a company can use to keep its data and software secure as well as accessible. A cloud architect develops a blueprint of the ideal cloud-hosting system for the organization. The architect works with a provider, such as Microsoft Azure or Amazon Web Services (AWS), to hire its servers, hardware, and other technical needs for the cloud

---

A Few Facts

Number of Jobs
About 50,248 in 2019

Median Pay
$141,037 in 2019

Educational Requirements
Bachelor's degree in computer science or similar field

Personal Qualities
Flexible, organized, task oriented

Work Settings
In an office; may include travel to clients

Future Job Outlook
Projected 9 percent growth through 2024

---

system. Once the blueprint is approved, the architect focuses on ensuring that the cloud model is developed as designed and that the company's information is successfully migrated to the cloud storage system. Sometimes the architect might purchase access to a suite of software hosted on a cloud server so that the company itself does not need to invest in the software. When the appropriate cloud solution is implemented, the architect will continue to ensure it is working as expected and tweak it as needed.

Cloud solutions architects can work directly for a single employer on that particular company's cloud architecture, or they might work for a cloud solutions provider and therefore serve multiple customers. Cloud solutions architects might work on all different phases of a cloud model at once, or they may be focused specifically on areas such as design, implementation, or improvements. Whatever their employment and focus, cloud solutions architects will ensure that any information stored in the cloud will be easy to access and safe from intrusion.

A Typical Workday

A cloud solutions architect's day is varied, with multiple types of tasks and goals always on the schedule. If the architect works for a cloud services provider, he or she will spend part of the day meeting with customers who require a cloud solution. These meetings might be conducted in person or through conference calls; the purpose is to determine a client's needs. At these meetings, the client will discuss requirements, such as what type of data and applications need to be stored, how much storage is needed, and how many people need to have access. The architect and client will also discuss whether the cloud provider has software that the customer would like to use or whether the client wants the ability to create software in the cloud network.

The next step for solutions architects is to design the technical plans for the cloud set up. Designing entails determining the types and number of databases and servers required, the power needed by computer processing units, and the types of wireless

9

connections needed to access the cloud. If an architect works with a specific cloud provider, such as AWS or Azure, then he or she designs the cloud model using the networks, servers, and software these companies provide. Typically, these providers are always advancing the technologies and capabilities they offer. Matt, an AWS cloud architect, says, "Every day it's an evolution being able to take advantage of those new features and functionality."[2]

Cloud architects work closely and meet with solutions engineers, who are typically the ones that actually set up the cloud environments after architects design them. An architect needs to meet with the engineer during the design phase to ensure the engineer understands the specifications and can meet them. The two professionals also work together to determine the best way to migrate the data and software the company wants to place in the cloud system. Once implemented, a solutions architect often reviews existing environments to see what is working and what is not, such as how quickly data is being processed. The architect then strives to correct all shortcomings.

Because customer needs are different and the architect's solutions vary, the job remains challenging. Each day includes a new set of problems and tasks. Maria, an AWS cloud architect, says, "You never know what you're going to be doing the next day and that's what excites me."[3]

Education and Training

Cloud services providers as well as private companies with an IT staff want to hire cloud architects who have a bachelor's degree in IT, computer science, or a related field. To reach that goal, high school students should take higher-level math courses, along with any computer science classes that are offered. However, even those without a degree can get into the field if they are willing to make an effort to learn.

For instance, industries are often more inclined to hire a person who has obtained a certification for cloud architecture. Even without a degree in computer science or a related field, a person can still obtain certification. The AWS Certified Solutions Architect, Google Cloud Certified Professional, and Microsoft's Azure Solutions Architect are among the certifications available. These certifications include taking a course (some classes are offered online) and passing a certification test.

Skills and Personality

Because they often interact with clients and coworkers, cloud architects should have well-developed communication skills allowing them to speak and write clearly, directly, and persuasively. Being flexible is also necessary, since architects may be determining how to migrate data one moment and then meeting with a customer to set up requirements the next. Also, being task oriented is beneficial because most architects are on a schedule and need to complete specific work by specific deadlines.

As for skills, cloud architects must understand the building blocks of IT. These basics include client systems and applications, networking, infrastructure, data centers, programming languages, web tools and technologies, databases, and big data. According to the website of New Horizons Computer Learning Centers, "Becoming a cloud architect is easier when you already have a technical background. Cloud architects need to understand which cloud vendors and tools will work best for a company's needs. They also need to know how to communicate with vendors to negotiate contracts for software, hardware and other cloud technologies."[4]

A cloud architect and solutions engineer share ideas during the design phase of their project. Their goal is to find the best way to migrate a company's data and software to their cloud system.

Working Conditions

Cloud solutions architects typically work in an office at a company; some might work from home since the job chiefly entails working on digital solutions for a company. Either way, cloud architects have a dedicated area with a computer or computers in order to access particular cloud platforms such as Azure or AWS. Throughout the day, they interact with others either in person or via conference calls, or they may travel to visit customers. Most architects work full time and may work extra hours as they get closer to implementation of a storage solution or migration of client data. They might also have to put in overtime to resolve any issues with these activities.

Employers and Pay

According to *Forbes*, as of 2019, there were 50,248 cloud computing positions available in the United States from 3,701 employers. Of the employers, Oracle, Deloitte, and Amazon had the most cloud computing jobs available that year. Additionally, most cloud computing employees in 2019 were based in Chicago, New York, San Francisco, San Jose, and Washington, DC—places where many of the largest employers have offices.

Because of the great demand for cloud computing architects, the pay is high. According to Salary.com, the average cloud solutions architect salary in the United States was $141,037 as of August 2019. The full pay range at the time fell between $122,365 and $158,944.

What Is the Future Outlook for Cloud Solutions Architects?

Cloud solutions architects are in demand by many companies. According to a 2018 study by Gartner, a leading research and advisory company, the public cloud market accounted for more than $186 billion in revenues in 2018. By 2021 the total revenue for cloud computing services is expected to exceed $300 billion. Because of this, LinkedIn has reported that "cloud and distributed computing" topped the list of sought-after skills in both 2016 and 2017. Additionally, Dice.com reported that job listings for the AWS cloud platform increased by 76 percent from 2015 to 2016.

The rise stems from a change in how businesses store information and data, says Paul Wallenberg, senior unit manager of technology services at staffing and recruiting firm LaSalle Network. He told TechRepublic, "As companies move away from an

Different Each Day

"For me every single day is different and brings a lot of change and learnings with it. Normally I visit customers and work with them in workshops for their Datacenter and Cloud designs, help our sales team in presales or do presentations at Microsoft events and communities all over the world, which is awesome."

—Thomas Mauer, cloud architect for itnetX, a consulting and engineering company based in Switzerland

Quoted in IT Camp, "Interview with Thomas Mauer," 2019. https://itcamp.ro.

on-premise infrastructure model to a cloud-first approach when upgrading or designing new environments, the need to hire technologists with cloud experience has increased dramatically."[5] The high number of jobs means that people with any type of cloud computing skills are in demand to fill these listings.

Find Out More

AWS Certified Solutions Architect Professional
http://aws.amazon.com/certification/certified-solutions-architect-professional

Amazon provides specific information on how to become certified as an AWS Solutions Architect. It details the topics covered in the course and indicates how to enroll. Additionally, the site provides links to other AWS courses.

Azure Blog
https://azure.microsoft.com/en-in/blog

This blog provides the latest information about Azure cloud technology. It contains articles about its systems, tools, and products. It also provides links to all types of training that Azure offers, including certification courses.

Cloud Tweaks
www.cloudtweaks.com

This website provides articles on the latest developments in cloud technology and business. The article topics range from those that focus on specific technologies to how specific types of businesses use and benefit from cloud computing.

InfoWorld Cloud Computing
www.infoworld.com/category/cloud-computing

On this website, visitors can read articles, videos, reviews, and news on all aspects of cloud computing. The articles provide information on the future of cloud computing, comparisons of cloud providers, cloud strategies for businesses, and more.

Computer Vision Engineer

What Does a Computer Vision Engineer Do?

In Norfolk, Virginia, computer vision technology is helping reunite lost dogs and cats with their owners. When staff members at a local shelter find a lost pet, they take a picture of it and place the picture on Finding Rover, a separate company website. Anyone who loses a dog or cat can also submit a photo to Finding Rover, and the site's facial recognition technology will search for a match with any of the animals in its registry. If the program finds a match, the owner is notified and can be reunited with his or her pet.

Developing and programming facial recognition software is just one aspect of computer vision engineering. The field and its technology are used in a host of other decision-making tasks, such as checking the quality of auto parts in a manufacturing plant or diagnosing health issues by reading imaging scans. Computer vision engineers develop techniques to allow computers to "see" and understand digital images and videos and then make decisions based on a program's interpretation of the content.

Teaching a computer program how to interpret the image is the real challenge of computer vision engineering. "All a computer 'sees' is a matrix . . . of an image. A computer has no idea how to take these pixel

A Few Facts

Number of Jobs
About 31,700 in 2018

Median Pay
$118,370 in 2018

Educational Requirements
Bachelor's degree in computer science or similar field

Personal Qualities
Analytical, mathematical, logical

Work Settings
Office, indoors

Future Job Outlook
Projected 19 percent growth through 2026

intensities and derive any semantic [logical] meaning from the image,"[6] explains Adrian Rosebrock, a computer vision expert. This means computer vision engineers must teach the computer how to learn to recognize an image. A vision engineer will develop an algorithm—a digital set of instructions—that teaches the computer program how to find features on an image and use these features to determine what the image is. For example, a computer vision engineer will upload millions of photos of rabbits to the computer, and then use the algorithm to teach the computer program to learn the different features that make up a rabbit from its assessment of the photos. The computer should then be able to identify an image of a rabbit from what it has learned.

Computer vision engineers program the computer models and algorithms used both to interpret and make decisions based on the images. They create these algorithms using tools like MATLAB (a mathematical computing environment and programming language) and Python (another programming language) to process and analyze large amounts of data from images. They then use these programs to make decisions based on the data. Thus, a computer might determine two images are of the same person based on similar data collected from each photo: the distance between the eyes, the location of a visible mole, the length and shape of the ear, and so on.

A Typical Workday

Computer vision engineers offer services to a variety of industries, including retail, security, and health. In these industries, a computer vision engineer will work with clients to determine what services are needed. For instance, the police department might use computer vision to identify license plates on tollways, find the owner in a database, and automatically bill the vehicle owner for unpaid tolls. In such cases the computer vision engineer spends a good part of the day developing algorithms to teach a computer how to obtain the images and what decisions to make based on them.

Once the algorithms are developed and put into place, computer vision engineers then test them and tweak as needed. Lino Coria, a computer vision engineer at a retail company, works on a team to create algorithms that measure the size of people's feet based on their photos. "I develop computer vision algorithms that analyze images in order to identify and measure human body parts. I also test the performance of these algorithms. I work closely with bio-mechanical, design, hardware, and software engineers,"[7] explains Coria of his work at Wiivv, a custom fit footwear company.

While some vision engineers like Coria work with one company on its projects, others work as consultants and are hired on a contract basis by companies. Rosebrock, a computer vision expert who has created his own image search engines, has worked with many interesting organizations. "I've consulted with the National Cancer Institute to develop methods to automatically analyze breast [tissue] images for cancer risk factors,"[8] Rosebrock gives as one example. He finds his daily projects varied because he works for different clients.

Whether working for one organization or as a contractor, the goal of computer vision engineers is to benefit businesses or organizations with their work. Shahmeer Mirza, senior research and development engineer at Frito-Lay, achieved this by developing a computer vision model that predicts the weight of potatoes being processed during the chip manufacturing process. Mirza's system uses a camera and an algorithm to determine the weights.

This model led to significant savings for the company because it no longer had to spend money on equipment to weigh the potatoes. Like Mirza, computer vision engineers throughout the world are advancing the capabilities and applications of computer vision technology.

Education and Training

Companies expect computer vision engineers to have a bachelor's or advanced degree in computer vision, computer science, mathematics, machine learning, or related field. A higher-level degree leads to a greater chance of obtaining senior-level computer vision jobs. To prepare for the career, high school students should take algebra and calculus and learn computer languages such as Python, Java, and C++. Also, reading the latest publications about deep learning and computer vision will provide a basic understanding of how the field is changing.

Gaining practical experience with algorithms and computer vision programming will give individuals a much better chance of getting hired as a computer vision engineer. Newcomers can practice programming by using OpenCV, an open-source (free-to-use) library of programming functions used for real-time computer vision. "OpenCV is prebuilt with all the necessary techniques and algorithms to perform several image and video processing tasks. It's quite easy to use and this makes it clearly the most popular computer vision library on the planet!"[9] writes Aaron Lazar, a technology writer with Packt, a website providing technology news and tutorials.

Skills and Personality

Computer vision engineers must have strong technical skills, including the ability to understand programming and engineering in order to develop algorithms. The capability to understand high-level mathematical models is also a must because many of the algorithms and programs use these models. "There's also increasing demand for a different skill set that includes familiarity with [artificial intelligence] techniques as well as [business] expertise,"[10] says Brandon Purcell, an analyst at Forrester, a technology market research company.

As for personal traits, computer vision engineers must be analytical thinkers and be able to come up with different ways to solve problems. After all, the job is about helping an organization solve problems and using computer vision to do so.

Working Conditions

Computer vision engineers might work in an office or a lab, depending on what specific work they are doing. In either case, computer vision engineers will have access to the latest computer systems with fast processing speeds. Because they are working with images and videos, they will likely have digital cameras, scanners, and video equipment of the highest caliber. Depending on what industry they are working with, computer vision engineers may be working with 3-D printers, MRI and X-ray machines, or manufacturing equipment.

While at work, computer vision engineers keep up with the latest research, advance their own projects, and collaborate with peers. "Every other day, somebody will point me to some new paper that appeared on arXiv (a repository of technical articles) and I might invest an hour going through it. Once every few days, I'll meet colleagues to discuss progress on the sub-system we are responsible for, brainstorm new ideas if we're stuck on something,"[11] says Zeeshan Zia, a computer vision engineer working on self-driving cars. The switch between individual research time and collective work time helps keep the job interesting for most vision engineers.

Employers and Pay

Computer vision engineers can be found working for a variety of companies. In the health field, for example, they find ways to analyze X-rays for abnormalities. In government security, they identify potential contraband aboard cargo ships. The applications for computer vision are growing and getting more diverse every day, and computer vision engineers can find a place in almost any industry.

Because of the demand for computer vision engineers and the need for them to have an advanced education, the salary is relatively high. According to the Bureau of Labor Statistics, the mean pay for computer information and research scientists was $118,370 in 2018, and computer vision engineers fall into this category.

What Is the Future Outlook for Computer Vision Engineers?

Computer vision jobs are in demand, and this demand is growing as the technology advances and companies discover uses for that technology. Computer vision engineer took the number thirteen spot on Indeed's 2018 list of the best jobs in the United States. "My prediction is that over the next 10–20 years we will see a substantial number of computer vision apps and technologies launched," writes Rosebrock, who has spent his entire adult life working in computer vision. "Some will fail, others will succeed; but it will no doubt push computer vision farther (and faster) than it's ever been before."[12]

A report by Tractica, a technology market analysis firm, supports Rosebrock's findings. The report suggests that the computer vision industry (including software, hardware, and services) will grow from $1.1 billion in 2016 to $26.2 billion by 2025 because of advancements in connectivity and the ability of engineers to develop more advanced programs. As industries see the possibilities of computer vision and invest in it, career opportunities will remain high.

Find Out More

Computer Vision News

www.rsipvision.com/computer-vision-news

This magazine provides monthly online articles dedicated to computer vision. The magazine focuses on the latest developments and achievements in the field. It also features interviews with computer vision engineers, highlighting how they got into the field and their current work.

Machine Learning Mastery

https://machinelearningmastery.com

This website provides a basic explanation for computer vision and how it works. It also maintains a blog that discusses various computer vision issues. Step-by-step guides for understanding and learning computer vision are also available to download.

OpenCV

www.opencv.org

OpenCV is an open-source computer vision and machine learning software library that anyone can access. The library has more than twenty-five hundred cataloged algorithms. People can download and work with OpenCV without licensing the product.

PYImage

www.pyimagesearch.com

This is the website of Adrian Rosebrock, a computer vision expert who consults for companies and has created his own computer vision apps. He provides access to books about computer vision as well as tutorials regarding OpenCv and Python.

Cybersecurity Analyst

What Does a Cybersecurity Analyst Do?

Cybersecurity analysts protect organizations from unauthorized access to their digital information. Such threats multiply each day as more hackers discover ways to break into information systems. To defend against these threats, cybersecurity analysts determine where the computer security weaknesses are and eliminate them.

Without cybersecurity analysts, companies and organizations are at risk of having their data compromised. For example, in August 2019 Capital One Financial Corporation made public that the personal data of about 100 million customers and credit card applicants had been illegally accessed by a hacker. Other financial institutions and businesses have been breached over the years with similar accessing of customer data. Even US voting machines have been hacked, leaving many Americans feeling that democracy has been undermined.

To prevent cyberattacks, companies hire cybersecurity analysts to find and analyze vulnerabilities within an organization's information technology (IT) setup, including hardware, software, networks, and devices. Once the weak spots are identified, cybersecurity analysts create or patch security systems—such as firewalls and data

A Few Facts

Number of Jobs
About 112,300 in 2018

Median Pay
$98,350 in 2018

Educational Requirements
Bachelor's degree in cybersecurity or related field; CISSP certification recommended

Personal Qualities
Detail oriented, innovative, analytical

Work Settings
Indoors, in an office

Future Job Outlook
Projected 32 percent growth through 2028

encryption programs—to protect a client's computer networks. After implementation, the analysts institute and maintain security standards and teach those within the organization how to follow the standards.

A Typical Workday

Each day hackers develop new ways to breach IT systems, prompting cyber experts to create new protection methods. Leigh-Anne Galloway is a cybersecurity resilience leader at Positive Technologies, a company that provides cybersecurity to organizations. She starts her day by learning about the latest cyber threats and how to defend against them. "I read the major newspapers [as I commute to work] and look at the news feed on LinkedIn," she says. "In addition to this, I follow several people in security via their personal blogs and twitter."[13] This is part of Galloway's daily routine because the information changes rapidly.

Galloway is involved in marketing her company's cybersecurity capabilities to potential customers, while also ensuring that current customers' computer systems are kept secure. She may focus her mornings on marketing tasks, such as setting up a demonstration for a potential client to show how her company can protect the client's website from intrusion. She says, "Depending on the day, my afternoon could involve a mixture of meeting customers looking to secure their applications and infrastructure against modern day attacks [and attending] internal meetings or [doing] research. My job is really varied, so it's hard to predict exactly what will happen week by week."[14]

As opposed to marketing to new clients, cybersecurity analyst Jim Treinen's entire day is focused primarily on assessing and preventing threats to current clients of his company, ProtectWise. His days range from calm to hectic depending on what he inherits from his coworkers on a previous shift. "We never know what is going to happen. A day can start out calm or start out on fire and very quickly go from one or another,"[15] says Treinen. After getting a briefing on any suspicious incidents, Treinen has to determine what part of the network to watch closely for any potential attacks and then determine what can be done to prevent them.

Similarly to Treinen, Pavi Ramamurthy, who has worked in cybersecurity for over fifteen years, tries to prevent security incidents and deals with incidents when they occur. Ramamurthy loves both planning to protect a system from attacks and dealing with incidents. "I love building a wide variety of security programs, or just being in the thick of a security incident and driving the incident response process," Ramamurthy says. "Each comes with its own set of excitement and challenges. It's fulfilling to brainstorm with my team on ways to improve, and also keep up-to-date on security news, professionals and new technologies."[16] For Ramamurthy and others in the business, cybersecurity is an exciting field because each day there are new challenges.

Education and Training

Many companies prefer cybersecurity analysts to hold a bachelor's degree in cybersecurity or a similar field. High school students can prepare by taking programming and computer science courses, along with higher-level math classes that will be required to major in these fields.

However, because many companies are in immediate need of analysts, interested individuals need not major in cybersecurity. "Ideally, a major in computer science provides the foundation," says Candy Alexander, a cybersecurity consultant. "There are a lot of programs around information security or information assurance; there are even master's and doctorate degrees in this area. But if you're driven and passionate about cybersecurity, you can come from any background."[17]

There are certifications available for those interested in advancing in the field, and these will help anyone, whether the person has a degree in the field or not, to qualify for advanced jobs. The Certified Information Systems Security Professional (CISSP) is granted by the International Information System Security Certification Consortium. This certification is well respected and even required by some companies. To obtain it, analysts must possess a minimum of five years of direct full-time security work, take the CISSP course, and pass a test.

Skills and Personality

Cybersecurity analysts must have technical knowledge to understand threats to IT systems and the ways to protect against them. This knowledge includes programming skills and an understanding of hardware, software, networks, and cloud computing.

Cybersecurity analysts are analytical and decisive, and their personalities typically reflect this. According to Randall Frietzsche, chief information security officer for Denver Health, "The majority of folks in cyber security are analysts, who will analyze risk, they'll analyze threat intelligence, and they'll consolidate that intelligence into [actions] for your organization. Their job is to help the organization understand what is going on, and where the organization needs to be going."[18]

Cybersecurity analysts must assess threats and quickly implement well-thought-out plans to tackle them. They must also be adaptable and remain calm when dealing with threats and incidents. Still, the thrill of taking action against threats is what motivates these individuals. Jeremy Trinka, a cybersecurity expert, attests, "The constant change of pace keeps our adrenaline going and fuels our desire to learn and adapt. We work the best under pressure, especially when the stakes are high."[19]

Working Conditions

Cybersecurity analysts work in offices, either at a given company as an employee or at home as a contractor. Whether working on-site or off-site, cybersecurity analysts will typically have digital access to the organization's network to monitor and protect its systems. Most will have a wide array of tools to accomplish these tasks. For example, analysts may use Nmap, a network scanner that can find hosts and services on a computer, and Aircrack-ng, a set of software tools that is used to simulate Wi-Fi attacks to determine weaknesses in Wi-Fi networks. Analysts may use encryption tools such as KeePass and Password Safe to protect privacy on systems and install firewalls. Throughout the day, analysts may also conduct meetings or workshops with employees of the organization to explain to them what is needed to protect the company's systems.

Working in cybersecurity can require long days. If a security incident occurs, analysts may need to work on it until the system is secured. However, many say the long hours are offset by the excitement of the job and working with motivated people. "I get to work with really smart people every day, and my work is creative and dynamic,"[20] says Galloway.

Employers and Pay

Cybersecurity analysts are in demand. Firms are competing for good analysts and offer good pay and benefits to get qualified individuals. "It's a full-on war for cyber talent," said Matt Comyns, a managing partner at executive search firm Caldwell Partners, which specializes in information security. "[Chief executive officers] know that, so they play hardball. Everyone's throwing money at this."[21]

Governmental bodies, financial industries, and health care organizations are in particular need of cybersecurity experts to defend their sensitive and critical data. Additionally, small and medium-sized businesses are finding more need for cybersecu-

A cybersecurity analyst searches for vulnerabilities in hardware, software, networks, and devices. If vulnerabilities are found, the analyst will make security patches or come up with a plan for protecting the company's computer system.

rity experts as they adopt cloud services, which requires protection of data and information.

As industries realize the growing threats, they also realize the need for cybersecurity professionals to keep their systems and data secure, so the demand for cybersecurity experts is increasing. Because they are in such demand, cybersecurity analysts are well paid. According to the Bureau of Labor Statistics (BLS), the median salary of security analysts in 2018 was $98,350.

What Is the Future Outlook for Cybersecurity Analysts?

Cybersecurity is a growing field; according to the BLS, jobs are projected to grow 32 percent through 2028, which is much faster

Skills Cybersecurity Analysts Need to Have

"Good communication skills are always a must. [Written documentation of threats and actions] is a major part of what we do for our customers. A strong technical background [in] hardware, operating systems and networks [is] also required. Skills in troubleshooting, problem solving, research and multitasking are also highly recommended."

—Steve Moulden, information assurance analyst

Quoted in Utica College, "A Day in the Life of an Information Security Professional," 2019. https://programs.online.utica.edu.

than the average growth for all occupations. The demand is high because hackers are continually finding new ways to steal important information or make malicious attacks on organizations' computer networks. The threats are so great that the US government established the Cybersecurity and Infrastructure Security Agency in 2018 to protect critical infrastructure from physical and cyber threats.

Cybersecurity analysts are in demand to help defend against such threats and attacks. And because every business, organization, and government entity has grown dependent on the internet for communication, commerce, and information storage, it is clear that cybersecurity will remain a fast-growing field for the foreseeable future.

Find Out More

Cyber Defense Magazine
www.cyberdefensemagazine.com

This web magazine includes articles on the latest cybersecurity news and research papers detailing predictions for what will be occurring in the cybersecurity field. Additionally, the site hosts videos detailing information for cybersecurity professionals on many topics.

Cybrary

www.cybrary.it

The Cybrary website includes information on cybersecurity careers and offers online classes to help students gain knowledge for these careers. On the site are blogs, forums, and up-to-date news about cybersecurity and its professions.

National Cybersecurity Center (NCC)

https://cyber-center.org

The NCC is a nonprofit organization located in Colorado Springs, Colorado, that shares cybersecurity information. Its website provides links to cyber events that people can attend and information on how to establish a student NCC chapter.

Women in Cyber Security

www.wicys.org

This organization is focused on bringing together women in the cybersecurity professions to share their knowledge and experiences. The group's website has news about women in cybersecurity, webinars, ways to create a student chapter, and links to scholarship opportunities.

Data Scientist

What Does a Data Scientist Do?

When users log in to websites, they may see pop-up ads that seem particularly tailored to their lives. A scuba diver may see an ad for a mask while visiting Amazon, or a hiker may discover hiking boots advertised on his or her Facebook feed. These ads are not chosen at random; they have been selected by a computer algorithm—a digital set of instructions—that mines data from sources such as Facebook "likes" and posts or previous purchases on merchant sites. On the basis of this data, the algorithm chooses an ad that reflects a person's interests and places it on a website the person visits. Setting the algorithm up and developing programs to mine the data is the work of a data scientist.

Data scientists do significantly more than help retail companies advertise to customers, however. They work with governments and organizations of all types, including national and international agencies. For example, when the Ebola virus outbreak spread in West Africa in 2014, data scientists were able to help the World Health Organization collect information, analyze it, and use it to predict other areas that were at risk of being hit by the virus. This allowed global health officials to route supplies to the

> ### A Few Facts
>
> **Number of Jobs**
> About 31,700 in 2018
>
> **Median Pay**
> $118,370 in 2018
>
> **Educational Requirements**
> Master's degree in mathematics or similar field
>
> **Personal Qualities**
> Analytical, mathematical, detail oriented
>
> **Work Settings**
> Office setting
>
> **Future Job Outlook**
> Projected 16 percent growth through 2028

at-risk areas and warn populations of the danger. These actions reduced the spread of the deadly disease.

To accomplish their work, data scientists use programming tools to collect and organize data. Data scientists then use tools such as SAS, an analytic software program, to find trends in the data. Then, by running the data through algorithms, data scientists implement other programs to make decisions based on the trends. For example, data scientists working for Uber Eats have created algorithms that predict food delivery times to customers on the basis of the latest traffic and weather data.

Data scientists like those at Uber Eats work closely with businesses to understand their goals and then develop computer models to interpret data and make decisions to achieve these goals. Jason Goodman, a data scientist, explains how he views the role of data science:

> Data science came about as a compromise between research science roles and business analyst roles. The former used powerful methods but only indirectly influenced business decisions while the latter directly influenced business owners but wielded limited tools to do so. Data scientists make the most impact when they combine *both* sides together, mixing deep domain knowledge with the right statistical and engineering tools to make better decisions or useful data products.[22]

A Typical Workday

Combining data science and business is how Kira Radinsky found success as cofounder and chief technology officer of SalesPredict. Her company uses data analytics to help other companies determine where to focus their sales efforts to get better results. Radinsky is heavily involved in both marketing to clients and working on the algorithms SalesPredict uses. Her clients include companies from all industries, but she will only take on a client after a favorable evaluation of the quality of the client's data. "The most important thing is not the industry—different industries just require different data sets," Radinsky explains. "The companies need a certain number of sales wins and losses for our systems to predict accurately and they need to have organized information."[23]

Marco Michelangeli is a data scientist at Hopenly, a company that provides data analysis to business customers. Like Radinsky, he works to help clients make better business decisions. His day is mainly focused on data collection and analysis. Part of his day includes collecting data and cleaning it. *Cleaning data* is a term used to describe tasks such as filling or deleting empty cells in a data table and removing duplicate entries. He then analyzes the data and determines the simplest and most efficient way to generate the needed predictions for a customer. "Data Science is about solving problems, not building models. . . . Do not frustrate yourself over complex machine learning models: be simple, be helpful,"[24] recommends Michelangeli.

Because he works with clients from different types of businesses, Michelangeli works with varied data sets that require different solutions. This results in new tasks each day, which he loves. "I do not really have a routine, and this is the best thing about being a data scientist!" he says. "Every day it is different, a new challenge comes up and a new problem sits there waiting to be solved. I am not just talking about coding, math and statistics, but about the complexity of the business world."[25]

Education and Training

Most companies prefer to hire data scientists with advanced degrees. According to KDnuggets, a leading website on big data, 88 percent of data scientists have at least a master's degree, and 46 percent have a PhD. These degrees were most commonly in mathematics and statistics (32 percent), followed by computer science (19 percent) and engineering (16 percent). High school students can prepare for a future career in data science by taking

Finding New Insights into Business Operations

"Sharing results and interpretations of predictive models with a [subject matter expert in a business area] is always a fun experience. Maybe 10 percent of the insights you come up with from the interpretation of the model are things they hadn't heard or thought of before. That tends to be the interesting part of the exercise for them, and is pretty rewarding for me too."

—Randy Carnevale, director of data science at Capital One, a banking company

Quoted in Data Science Weekly, "Capital One Labs—Data Science at a Bank: Randy Carnevale Interview." www.datascienceweekly.org.

advanced courses in all areas of mathematics, including statistics and calculus, as well as programming courses.

Additionally, certifications can help those looking to obtain data scientist jobs. Microsoft offers certification as an Azure Data Scientist Associate, which requires one to three years of Azure experience, attending a training course, and passing an exam. Similarly, the analytic software company SAS offers its SAS Certified Data Scientist, which is available to students who complete eighteen online courses and pass five separate exams.

Skills and Personality

Data scientists must be able to combine extensive computer and mathematical knowledge to create and implement mathematical models and algorithms. They also need analytical aptitude, since they work to achieve business solutions. "In essence it requires an analytical mind," explains Colin Nugteren, chief analytics officer and data scientist at SAS. "Next to that, it is very useful to understand computers and data and the way they work together, because all major analytical advances are highly dependent on these systems."[26]

The ability to understand and solve problems and answer business questions are a major part of data scientists' jobs. "Those of us working in industries are hard-nosed problem solvers. Companies hire us not because they want to have a statistician on staff;

they hire us to solve problems, to create business value,"[27] says Daymond Ling, a data scientist for over twenty years at CIBC, a banking company. Being able to communicate clearly is also a necessity, since data scientists cannot suggest a solution if they cannot explain their reasoning or how it will benefit a client. For this reason, the ability to communicate verbally and in written form is crucial.

Working Conditions

Data scientists may work directly for a company to help achieve its business goals, or they may work for a consulting company that provides solutions to many different clients. Those who work for a single company will spend most of their time in the office, directly meeting with people at the company to understand requirements. Those working for consulting firms may spend time visiting customers at their companies to assess their needs and possibly work at those sites to access their data. Wherever they work, their days will be filled with technical work as well as meetings and consultations. "As with any high activity job, a data scientist has to juggle . . . a lot of presentations during the day. The results acquired from categorizing and analyzing data need to be presented to the stakeholders in a very efficient manner,"[28] writes Audrey Throne, a technology blogger.

When not in meetings, data scientists are in cubicles or offices working on finding solutions and recommendations for business problems or questions. Whiteboards, computers, programming tools, and software for modeling and analyzing are the tools of most data scientists. They will work with these throughout the day when dealing with data collection and analysis.

Employers and Pay

From health organizations to manufacturing industries, businesses are finding the benefits of using data science to become more efficient and profitable. Because of the high demand for data scientists, companies are willing to pay above-average salaries to hire them. Even data scientists who are just entering the field receive upper-level salaries. According to a 2018 study by Burtch Works, an executive recruiting firm, an entry-level data scientist's median starting salary was $95,000, and a mid-level data scientist's median salary was $128,750. On the highest end, an experienced data scientist salary was $165,000, with experienced management-level professionals considerably higher, at $250,000. Sticking with the profession, therefore, can bring financial rewards.

What Is the Future Outlook for Data Scientists?

Businesses are realizing the profit potential of data science. According to a 2018 research report by Gemalto, a data security company, 65 percent of the businesses polled said they could not analyze or categorize all of their data. Additionally, 89 percent of these companies realized that if they could analyze their information better, they would have a competitive edge. Because of this, a January 2019 report from Indeed, one of the top job sites, showed a 344 percent increase in demand for data scientists since 2013. Tied to this increased demand is a lack of qualified individuals. Therefore, individuals qualified in data science will have an excellent chance of finding a job in the field now and in the future.

Find Out More

Data Science Association
www.datascienceassn.org

The Data Science Association is a nonprofit professional association of data scientists, and its website provides information regarding current data science methodology. Also hosted on the site are podcasts, white papers, and videos about data science.

Discover Data Science
www.discoverdatascience.org

An informational website for those interested in data science, Discover Data Science provides basic information on the occupation, which degrees would assist with becoming a data scientist, and a discussion of common educational paths to acquire a degree. It also provides information on data science tools and how to use them.

365 Data Science
https://365datascience.com

This website provides information on what an aspiring data scientist should do to prepare for the field. It provides courses for free (though some advanced courses require a fee), and there is a blog with tutorials on programming and interviews with current data scientists.

Women in Data Science (WiDS)
www.widsconference.org

This is a website of an annual conference for women in data science. It provides information on the conference as well as podcasts featuring women currently working in the field. There are even videos of speeches from past conferences detailing the careers of women in data science.

Machine Learning Engineer

What Does a Machine Learning Engineer Do?

When someone says, "Alexa, add popcorn to my grocery list," they are probably not talking to a real person. They are most likely giving instructions to Amazon's Echo, the smart speaker that listens and responds to verbal commands through the personal assistant known as Alexa. The Echo is able to play music, make to-do lists, play audio books, give weather updates, and more after interpreting voice commands. What makes this possible is machine learning. What makes machine learning possible is the work done by machine learning engineers.

The extent of what machine learning can do is increasing each day. For example, machine learning is used in scientific exploration. Engineers at the Massachusetts Institute of Technology (MIT) and Woods Hole Oceanographic Institution have developed algorithms that give robotic boats the ability to locate and sample bodies of water where potentially hazardous chemicals might have been carried from a spill. "[The algorithm] leverages probabilistic techniques to predict which paths are likely to lead to the [site], while navigating obstacles, shifting currents, and other variables," explains Rob Matheson of MIT. "As it collects samples, it weighs what it's learned to

A Few Facts

Number of Jobs
About 31,700 in 2018

Median Pay
$111,911 in 2019

Educational Requirements
Master's degree in computer science or similar field preferred

Personal Qualities
Mathematical, persistent, logical

Work Settings
Indoors in an office

Future Job Outlook
About 2.3 million jobs globally by 2020

What Does It Take to Be a Machine Learning Engineer?

"Machine learning engineering is an interesting discipline. It requires being good at a variety of skills: obviously everything needed from a good data scientist, like curiosity, analytical skills, knowledge of algorithms, the ability to understand business requirements, and the need for good communication. But it also requires being good at software development—creating clean, maintainable software and systems."

—Shanif Dhanani, machine learning engineer

Shanif Dhanani, "A Day in the Life of a Machine Learning Engineer," Medium, March 23, 2018. https://medium.com.

determine whether to continue down a promising path or search the unknown—which may harbor more valuable samples."[29] All of this is accomplished without endangering the scientists.

These are just a few of the projects that utilize machine learning. In each, engineers create algorithms—sets of digital instructions that determine a process or function—that teach computers to adapt and respond appropriately to information. The computers use a base algorithm to analyze the information and create new algorithms based on what the machines have "learned." This is what allows these computers to interpret information and make decisions in ways that are similar to human decision-making.

A Typical Workday

Many machine learning engineers spend their days focused on solving business problems for companies. Chirag Mahapatra is an engineer at Airbnb, an online company that allows people a convenient means to rent their homes to travelers. He recently worked on a project to help Airbnb prevent fraud and other potential problems by using machine learning to help verify the identity and trustworthiness of people who use the company's online booking system. Part of Mahapatra's day includes meeting with people from the company's operations side to understand what they need from the verification system and how it could be improved. "I interact a lot with my product manager and our [operations] team to figure out what are the burning issues," he says. "What are we missing out there? Are we foreseeing incidents we could have prevented and figuring out how we can prevent them?"[30]

Like Mahapatra, Shanif Dhanani divides his day between meetings and programming. Dhanani is a cofounder and machine learning engineer at Apteo, a company that uses machine learning to help financial firms make better investment decisions and predictions. He meets with clients to see how his company's machine learning algorithms can help them. His day also includes checking the results of his artificial intelligence models used to analyze investment data. He reviews the results to ensure the models are making quality predictions. From there, he moves on to devise other algorithms or update existing ones. "We're continuing to research and improve our core [artificial intelligence] models," writes Dhanani, "while also investigating how new models and analytics can help investors to manage their investments."[31]

Similarly, Bhaskar Dhariyal spends the majority of his time developing and improving algorithms. Dhariyal works as a machine learning engineer at ION Energy, a company that uses machine learning to predict battery life. His responsibility is to develop advanced algorithms to identify causes of battery degradation and then suggest corrective measures to extend the battery's life. Part of his day is devoted to reading research papers on models, programming his models, and meeting with his manager and teams to discuss results. "The best part is, I'm always given the opportunity to experiment with my models, and my peers are open to listening to and implementing my ideas,"[32] says Dhariyal.

Education and Training

Students interested in machine learning should take mathematics courses and computer programming throughout their education. Obtaining an advanced degree is generally a necessity to work as a machine learning engineer. Employers expect applicants to have a bachelor's degree in computer science or similar field, but most prefer a master's or even a doctoral degree. Employers also tend to hire candidates who have computer programming experience.

Those currently in the field suggest that newcomers acquire training in other areas of information technology as well. Imran Hendley suggests that aspiring machine learning engineers learn about software engineering. "In my own path, it's been really helpful to have a strong foundation in software engineering," Hendley explains. "Because when you work in a company as a machine learning engineer, often you'll really have to understand the software product and kind of integrate your work into an existing software system."[33]

Prospective job candidates can also enhance their qualifications by obtaining certifications. One of the most sought after is the Machine Learning Certification by Stanford University. It involves a fifty-six-hour online course with quizzes and assignments.

Skills and Personality

Mathematical ability is a necessity because machine learning engineers develop algorithms that require an understanding of high-level math concepts, particularly in statistics and probability. Additionally, deep programming skills are needed to be able to develop algorithms and integrate them into computer systems.

As for character, engineers need persistence, since computer models often need to be changed and refined on the basis of their performance. Being detail oriented is also necessary, since algorithms need to be precise to be effective. Additionally, the field is rapidly changing, and machine learning engineers need to keep current on advancements in the field, so the ability to learn quickly is helpful. Lastly, like other careers that include interaction with customers, peers, and clients, being able to clearly communicate thoughts and ideas is beneficial.

Working Conditions

Many machine learning engineers work directly for companies and complete projects to help advance those companies' busi-

Communication Is Key

"Most of the major roadblocks I ran into [as a machine learning engineer] were not technical, they were communicative. Sure, there were always technical challenges, but that's the role of an engineer, to fix the technical challenges. Never underestimate the importance of communication, internal and external. There's nothing worse than solving a technical challenge when it was the wrong technical challenge to be solved."

—Daniel Bourke, former machine learning engineer at Max Kelsen, now a technology podcaster

Daniel Bourke, "12 Things I Learned During My First Year as a Machine Learning Engineer," KDnuggets, July 7, 2019. www.kdnuggets.com.

ness objectives. They typically work on-site in a dedicated office space. Others work for consulting companies that provide machine learning services to various companies, so these engineers may be involved in several different types of projects, depending on the clients. Working at a consulting company will likely require some travel to clients for meetings. In all situations, machine learning engineers will divide their day between reading to keep up with the latest machine learning advances, reviewing algorithm performance, programming algorithms, and meeting with team members and project managers. Because of the type of programming they do, machine learning engineers typically are provided computers with high-speed processors and the latest in software applications used for machine learning.

Machine learning engineers often work with others who have similar educations and interests in computers. This generally makes for an exciting environment in which high-level concepts are shared and discussed. Carolina Galleguillos, who has a PhD in computer science, talks about what she loves as a machine learning engineer at Thumbtack, an online company that matches customers with local service professionals. "The team," explains Galleguillos. "I love the energy here, the passion, and how smart people are. I learn a lot every day from the people I'm working with."[34]

Employers and Pay

Developing targeted customer marketing algorithms is a major focus of machine learning. For this reason, major companies that use machine learning include Facebook, Amazon, Google, and Uber. However, companies of all industries, from financial to manufacturing, are seeing the potential of machine learning. Because of this, machine learning engineer jobs can be found at small, midsize, and large companies in all types of industries.

Both the demand for machine learning engineers and the high educational requirements have resulted in lucrative salaries for those in the field. In 2019, according to PayScale, the average salary for a machine learning engineer was $111,911; Glassdoor placed the average at $121,321. Greater experience leads to even higher salaries, an incentive for those considering it as a long-term career.

What Is the Future Outlook for Machine Learning Engineers?

Machine learning engineers are in demand, and this demand is predicted to increase. In 2019 Indeed reported that there was a 344 percent growth in job postings for machine learning engineers from 2015 to 2018. Additionally, artificial intelligence, of which machine learning is a subset, was projected to have created 2.3 million jobs by 2020, according to a *Gartner Report*. International Data Corporation, a technology marketing firm, estimates that spending on machine learning and artificial intelligence is anticipated to have grown from less than $8 billion in 2016 to $47 billion by 2020.

Since machine learning requires highly skilled individuals with advanced educations, the job market is wide open. Vitaly Gordon, vice president of data science and software engineering for Salesforce Einstein, a company that provides technology software solutions, says, "Machine learning engineering is a discipline that requires production grade coding, PhD level machine learning, and the business acumen of a product manager. Finding such rare people can uplift a company from a follower into a leader in their space, and everyone is looking for them."[35] Those with drive, skills, and the ability to learn will find themselves a wide range of opportunities as a machine learning engineer.

Find Out More

Google AI
https://ai.google

A business site, Google AI focuses on different ways that artificial intelligence, specifically machine learning, is used in organizations and companies. It focuses on Google products, but there are different articles on the basics of machine learning and access to open source programs to practice machine learning for free.

Guru 99
www.guru99.com

Guru 99 is a website developed to allow people to learn technology for free. The website provides a machine learning tutorial that was developed to teach people the basics of machine learning. The website also includes a blog on the latest developments in machine learning technology.

Machine Learning Mastery
https://machinelearningmastery.com

For those interested in learning the basics of machine learning to those coding advanced algorithms, this website provides free "how to" articles. It was developed by Jason Brownle, a machine learning engineer. It also provides an FAQ section with basic to advanced questions.

Women in Machine Learning and Data Science (WIMLDS)
http://wimlds.org

The WIMLDS is a nonprofit organization dedicated to promoting women in machine learning and data science. The website posts news about the accomplishments of women working in these fields. It also includes a job search for machine learning and related careers as well as contacts of women in the field.

Mobile App Developer

What Does a Mobile App Developer Do?

Every day teens around the world check Snapchat or TikTok on their smartphones. Adults log in to their banking apps to pay bills or deposit checks. Kids play games like *Minecraft* or *Animal Jam* on their tablets. As of 2019, over 5 billion people in the world used mobile applications ("apps"), according to We Are Social, a global marketing firm. Mobile app developers are the ones who create these applications. They either build entirely new apps or modify applications used on laptops and desktops so the apps can be used on mobile devices.

Whether creating an app for a company or developing one to sell directly to users, a mobile app developer's goal is to build an application that is both easy to use and appealing. A mobile app developer has to consider both the design of the application's user interface (UI), which is what the users will interact with, and the back-end of the application, which is the programming that runs the application. Developers often are involved in the entire development cycle, so they must know how to design, program, test, and, at times, market their app.

Once the development phase is complete and the app is released, mobile app developers often feel a sense

A Few Facts

Number of Jobs
About 23 million worldwide in 2019

Median Pay
$92,721 in 2019

Educational Requirements
Bachelor's degree in computer science or similar field

Personal Qualities
Creative, technical, persistent

Work Settings
Shared or personal office

Future Job Outlook
Projected 19 percent growth through 2027

of accomplishment. Gregg Weiss is the chief executive officer and founder of Blue Whale Apps, a mobile app development company. He says that he never tires of seeing his company's apps impact people's lives. "It's rewarding to develop apps and see them live in the store with great ratings and know that what you had a hand in making has then affected someone else in a positive way," Weiss explains. "We released an iPad app called Speech Therapy for Apraxia that has great reviews and is consistently in the Top 25 Medical iPad apps. This is an app that can actually help kids with speech issues."[36]

After an app has gone public, an app developer often receives feedback and then modifies the programming to eliminate bugs and perhaps enhance the app to perform better or to expand its functions.

A Typical Workday

Ian Joyner is a member of the app development team at Apadmi, a company that creates apps for clients. His company has developed apps such as SailGP, which allows people to watch livestream sailing races on their phones. Once at work, Joyner dives into coding, particularly if his team is in the middle of app development. His tasks depend on what stage of the development his team has reached. Joyner, like many developers, is involved in all stages of app development. "This variety and influence at all stages of the project really appeals to me,"[37] he asserts.

Joyner also says that his day includes several meetings. He needs to understand the client's requirements and, as the project continues, to determine whether they are satisfied with the progress. This results in daily calls and face-to-face meetings every week or two. In addition to client meetings, Joyner gathers with his team often to discuss the status of the app, brainstorm solutions to any problems, and determine whether the members are meeting their deadlines.

Hussain Fakhruddin is an app developer at TeksMobile, a mobile app and game development company. Like Joyner, he finds meetings an important part of his day. Most days start with team meetings, in which everyone updates where they are on their part of development and what milestones are next. After attending the morning meeting and checking his email, Fakhruddin gets to coding. Most of his coding is in programming languages such as Objective-C or Swift, but which language he codes in depends on the requirements of the app. He notes, "I get a real kick out of coding the actual user-interface of new applications. The database and the backend support are all very important, but unless the UI is properly optimized—my app is not gonna work."[38]

For Fakhruddin and all developers, it is fulfilling to be a part of a project from the beginning until the end. Whether working alone or on a team, success is the release and use of their products.

Education and Training

Typically, employers want a mobile app developer who at least has a bachelor's degree in computer science, software engineering, or a similar field. High school students who aspire to become mobile app developers should consider taking programming, computer science, and graphics arts classes to prepare for both the technical and creative sides of app development.

Many companies also want to see that applicants have developed a portfolio of apps they have created on their own. Randle Browning, who is a content consultant to tech companies, suggests that those seeking mobile app jobs build a personal website to highlight their projects, from development to implementation. "If you built an app using JavaScript or jQuery, go beyond simply including a screenshot and link to the app itself. Put in screenshots of the mock-up you did when you were planning the app, how the app looked before you made it interactive,"[39] he recommends.

Learning marketable skills such as object-oriented programming, Java programming, C++ programming, and UI design also add to an aspiring mobile app developer's résumé. For a fee, these can be learned at on-site coding boot camps, where students learn to code a specific language quickly. Free and for-fee online courses in programming are also available.

Apps Tailored to the Customer

"I had to learn to walk in my customers' shoes and think about how my products and services touch the broad aspects of their lives. I needed to think about processes, tools, use cases, analyses and ripple effects far beyond the specific use of our app. What are my customers . . . trying to accomplish? What barriers are in the way? What opportunities can we provide that they don't yet recognize themselves?"

—Niel Nickolaisen, mobile app developer

Niel Nickolaisen, "Mobile App Development Process: Saving Time, Money," Tech Target, January 28, 2015. https://searchcio.techtarget.com.

Additionally, people can enhance their résumés if they take courses to acquire the Associate Android App Developer certification through the Google certification program or the Oracle Java ME Mobile Application Developer certification.

Skills and Personality

Mobile app developers should possess a creative mind-set, since they need to produce apps that visually appeal to people. They also should be detail oriented in order to program responses for all the different ways a user may interface (swiping, clicking, etc.) with the app. Being able to focus under pressure is also key to being a good developer because the work can result in long hours as deadlines approach. Tied to this is the ability to deal with problems as they arise and to work on these problems until a solution is found.

As for technical skills, mobile developers must understand programming languages such as Java and C++ to build apps. In addition, developers must be able to quickly learn the latest technology in order to be successful. "One of the increasingly challenging areas of being an app developer is the rapid changes to mobile operating systems that we see. There is a constant requirement to learn new aspects of languages,"[40] says Joyner.

Mobile app developers work together to create an app that will be appealing and easy to use. They will also need to make sure their programming enables the app to perform as intended and, if it does not, find a fix.

Working Conditions

The majority of mobile app developers work directly for companies that either create their own apps or provide apps for clients. These developers usually work on-site and follow a normal full-time workweek. However, others work as freelancers and are either hired by companies on a contract basis or develop and sell their own apps. Freelancers often work from home, and because of their flexibility, they can determine their own schedules, as long as they meet deadlines.

Whether at a company or working from home, developers spend a good portion of time at a desk, often working extra hours when deadlines loom. Different developers find ways to best adapt to the long hours. "I will be spending around 10–12 hours after this sitting in front of a Mac computer. It's essential that my static state does not compromise my physical fitness in the long run. I get out of home at 6:30 am sharp, go on a morning jog,"[41] says Fakhruddin. Others find listening to music through headphones as they work or stopping to take quick breaks is the best method for them. The day also is not all sitting and coding, since there are meetings and discussions with clients and colleagues. For most, enduring the long hours is not difficult because of the passion they have for developing apps and seeing the end result of their work.

Employers and Pay

Companies of all kinds hire mobile app developers or contract independent companies that specialize in mobile apps to develop apps that benefit their businesses. In 2019 the combination of those working for companies and those who freelanced resulted in an estimated 23 million people working as mobile app developers worldwide, according to Evans Data Corporation.

As with most technical fields, mobile app developers make a comparatively high salary. Glassdoor found that the average salary in 2019 for a mobile application developer was $92,721, while Indeed's September 2019 survey recorded an average of $112,646. Location and experience affect salary. For example, large tech cities like New York, Houston, and San Francisco offer higher salaries than the national average. Additionally, a mobile developer with higher levels of education related to the field and greater experience will generally make more than the average salary.

What Is the Future Outlook for a Mobile App Developer?

Mobile application use has grown extensively since apps came into existence in 2008. The growing use of apps is evident. Statista reports that in 2017 mobile users downloaded 178.1 billion apps on their devices, and that is expected to rise to 258.2 billion by 2022.

Because of the rising levels of app use, consumers are generating more revenue. Statista predicts that by 2021 the mobile

Importance of Apps to Industry

"The biggest change I've seen in the industry right now over the last year and a half is that businesses are actually seeing that they can use a mobile app to help either increase revenue, increase leads (potential clients) or decrease manpower [to] decrease costs."

—Jeremy Callahan, chief technology officer of Callahan and Associates, a mobile app development firm

Quoted in LAMA, "Interview with Jeremy Callahan," 2019. https://lama-app.com.

app market in the United States will rise to $820 billion in revenue. This should lead to an increase of people working as developers. In 2017 a CNNMoney/PayScale report predicted a 19 percent growth in the field by 2027. With these statistics, it is easy to see that qualified individuals can foresee a long-term career in the field.

Find Out More

Adobe Mobile App Development
www.adobe.com/devnet/devices/mobile-apps.html

The software giant Adobe devotes a section of its company website to mobile app development. Visitors can read about how to get started developing mobile applications for iOS and Android or with HTML and JavaScript. The website gives links to access user guides for building apps and to sample apps with the latest features.

Andrey Gordeev
https://andreygordeev.com

Andrey Gordeev is a freelance contractor who develops apps for iOS/Android businesses. This site showcases his personal portfolio, and visitors can see the different types of apps he has created, which include both a social network and a music app.

App Developers Alliance

https://appdevelopersalliance.org

The App Developers Alliance is a website that provides free guides, articles, news stories, and general advice on app development. It offers information geared to both the novice and the expert in app development. Additionally, the site includes reviews and links to the latest apps.

Developers Alliance

www.developersalliance.org

Developers Alliance is a nonprofit organization that provides developers of websites, software, and apps a way to keep up with the latest developments in their field. The website includes access to a blog, news articles about the industry, and research papers.

User Interface Designer

What Does a User Interface Designer Do?

When people use an app, video game, or website, what they see and how they interact with the screen constitutes the user interface (UI). The colors, words, pictures, icons, and backgrounds must be appealing, and the navigational tools—such as scroll bars and drop-down lists—must be easy to manipulate. These elements are planned by a UI designer, who strives to make the user's experience pleasant and rewarding so that the user will return to the site or reuse the app.

UI designers focus specifically on designing a look and layout of a product to give the user a positive experience. UI designers use patterns, spacing, and color to guide users through their experiences with the website or app. Hannah Alvarez, a designer with InVision, a company that provides digital design services to clients, explains, "The purpose of any interface is to help the user accomplish their goals. As a UI designer, your job isn't just to create something beautiful; it's to understand the user's mindset, predict what they will expect, and then make the design as user-friendly as possible."[42] Much of what a successful UI designer creates will go unnoticed by the user, however. That is, most users will not focus on the interface but instead enjoy the experience and function of the

A Few Facts

Number of Jobs
About 160,500 in 2019

Median Pay
$80,450 in 2019

Educational Requirements
Bachelor's degree in digital or graphic design or similar field

Personal Qualities
Intuitive, detail oriented, creative

Work Settings
Office setting

Future Job Outlook
Projected 13 percent growth through 2028

app or site. Thus, the ease of use of an interface is the hallmark of a good design.

To reach a good design, UI designers first meet with clients interested in creating an app, program, or website. The meeting will help determine the design requirements needed to make the program or site useful. Then the designers will start developing ideas for visuals, often beginning with sketches and "mood boards" (boards with different color schemes and design patterns) to get a feel for the look of the product. From there, they use software tools such as Sketch, Figma, and Adobe XD to design wireframes, which are visual mock-ups that outline the basic visual structure of the website, app, or program.

The next step includes making prototypes, using tools like InVision software, through which the visual aspect and UI of the product can be tested. After further meetings in which all involved discuss problems or ways to develop a better design, the design team will fix or update the interface. From there, the visual design is implemented into the final product by software engineers and programmers who do the actual coding.

A Typical Workday

Kyle Markell is a senior UI designer at Konrad, a company that provides digital design products. He starts his day by meeting with his team to ensure everyone is on the same design page and to brainstorm new ideas. Throughout the day, in between actual designing, he continues to reach out to those impacted by the design, including other designers and coding programmers. "My day . . . has multiple touchpoints with the teams, not limited to my own, to make sure things are moving at the required pace, also to test my solutions on others, gain outside perspective and have some iterative design sessions with some fellow designers,"[43] Markell explains.

Like Markell, Jennie M., a senior UI designer at ASOS, an online retailer, spends part of her day meeting with others, many of whom are online shoppers. "Our team is responsible for designing how the website and apps work," she says. "We talk to customers and make sure we can make the experience of shopping on ASOS as efficient, easy to use and functional as possible, so our customers can make informed choices."[44] She uses this information to maintain an appealing site interface.

When not in meetings, UI designers devote their time to actually designing the interfaces. Matt Bartlett is a senior UI designer at the web-design agency Ridgeway. He says his main priority is to translate the user's experience into combinations of color, arrangements of screens and levels, helpful images and icons, and lettering styles. "With all the necessary information at hand, I'll start crafting the interface of whichever solution I'm working on," Bartlett says. "In most cases, I'll be designing templates and components for desktop, tablet and mobile devices."[45]

Once the templates are drafted, Bartlett runs them by the programmers to ensure the visual plan can be translated into code. If the plan is feasible, the programmers integrate the design into the final product, and the UI designer can see the fully functional program, app, or website.

Education and Training

Most UI designers have a bachelor's degree in graphic or digital design because many companies prefer to see such a degree when hiring. While in high school, taking courses such as graphic arts, basic art, drawing, and anything art related will help prepare students to reach these educational goals.

Although it is easier to find a job in the field with a degree, people can still learn the basics of design on their own and find a path to a UI career. "You need to invest your time in acquiring knowledge and then making use of the knowledge you will gain, so start reading articles, books, listen to podcasts and watch design related videos," says Dawid Tomczyk, a self-taught senior UI designer. "There are tons of articles & video tutorials available online for you to learn about new design trends, use cases and tutorials."[46]

There are also UI design courses available from different companies and schools that lead to UI certifications. These add to one's knowledge and skill set, which is helpful when applying for a job in the field. An example of a certification is UI Design Specialization by California Institute of the Arts, which is earned by taking four online courses over sixteen weeks.

Skills and Personality

UI designers must possess creativity and imagination in order to craft an engaging interface. Additionally, designers must be intuitive so that they can understand how users feel when seeing and using elements of the product. Also, designers must be dedicated to the effort required to research and understand users. Steve Portigal, a design consultant on digital projects, explains, "It's incredibly important to be able to talk to people who might use your product—not just to get their critique of your solution, but before you even consider a solution. That's when you can have the most open mind and learn about their current behavior and the motivations that drive that behavior."[47]

Being detail oriented is also important, because designing is about the details. From the colors to the layout, every design choice impacts the user. "When it comes to UI . . . design attention to details is crucial—sometimes even really small and subtle change might make [a] huge difference, so you need to start paying attention to every single detail of your designs,"[48] explains Tomczyk.

While UI designers do not code extensively, technical skills—such as the ability to use software tools like InVision and Sketch to build visual wireframes and prototypes—are essential. Some coding knowledge also makes it easier for designers to communicate with programmers.

Working Conditions

UI designers may work as freelance designers from their home office or work at a company, often in a shared work space. Those who work on-site may work in offices that are designed to stimulate creativity and design. Rather than a typical cubicle or office setting, some companies, like IBM, find it beneficial to have their design teams work in open studio spaces. "On an average day in the studio, you'll likely find designers busy working at common tables surrounded by whiteboards and walls full of design artifacts. But, big open spaces might not be everyone's cup of tea all the time," explains Arin Bhowmick, global vice president of design at IBM. "Sometimes designers need a quiet place to work heads down or talk privately to a remote colleague or manager."[49]

UI designers will have access to design tools that allow them to build an interface. Since most of their work is on computers, they will typically have computers with large monitors to see their work clearly and have access to all the software tools for forming the prototypes.

Employers and Pay

UI designers are often directly employed by companies to develop websites, apps, and programs for clients. Apple, Google, IBM, and numerous other companies use UI designers to make their products look appealing and to convince consumers that these products are easy to use. A company's reputation often rests on how user-friendly their programs, apps, and sites are.

Because businesses recognize the importance of popular and useful interfaces, they are willing to pay higher-than-

User interface designers focus on what users see and how they interact with apps, video games, and websites. They use sketches and mood boards that have different color schemes and design patterns to get a feel for the look of on-screen visuals.

average salaries to UI designers. In 2019 Glassdoor reported $80,450 as the average salary of a UI designer. In the same year, ZipRecruiter found that annual salaries ranged from $23,500 to $161,000. However, the site noted that the majority of entry-level UI designer salaries fell in the range of $59,000 to $112,000.

What Is the Future Outlook for UI Designers?

Companies have found that increasing the quality of their technological products results in more profit, and good quality includes a sharp interface. Over the past decade, companies like Apple and Facebook have employed a design-centric mind-set to set themselves apart from the competition. This is why UI designers have a bright future. In fact, UI designer came in third as the most in-demand digital, marketing, and design role for

Keep Users Involved

"There are many ways to explain the reasoning behind your [UI design decisions], but the best and most efficient way to do it, in my experience, is to test it. The only way we can make sure we are meeting people's expectations is to do user testing. If your users understand your interactions, your mapping of elements, and the choices you've presented them; then you are successful."

—Kyle Markell, senior UI designer at Konrad

Kyle Markell, "On the Days I Wear My UI Cap," Medium, February 1, 2018. https://medium.com.

2019, according to recruiting firm Onward Search. Additionally, the Bureau of Labor Statistics projects that web developers, which includes UI designers, will have a 13 percent job growth rate through 2028. Thus, UI designers are likely to experience a higher-than-average growth in job availability over this time.

Find Out More

Good UI
www.goodui.org

Jakub Linowski, founder and editor of Good UI, developed this website to allow people to learn and talk about UI. A blog on this site discusses many subjects concerning UI designs, and another section offers reviews and updates for UI software. There are even sample templates that can be used for UI designs.

Learn UI Design
https://learnui.design

Created by a self-taught UI designer, this website provides online courses (for a fee) on UI. Topics include how to create a UI designer portfolio, ways to create a more exciting design, and different types of fonts and colors. It also provides free advice through blog postings.

Site Inspire

www.siteinspire.com

Site Inspire was developed to showcase high-quality UI designs of websites. People and organizations submit their websites, and the managers of Site Inspire choose those with the best designs to feature on the site. There are over seven thousand websites featured for users to search and view.

Usability

www.usability.gov

This is a government resource that provides UI guidelines and practices for people and companies creating designs for government use. Included on the website is an overview of the design process, a discussion of tools and methods used to create designs, and articles on specific UI topics that range from government website requirements to creating wireframes.

Virtual Reality Developer

What Does a Virtual Reality Developer Do?

Today it is possible for many people to visit new worlds or experience different realities without leaving the comfort of their living rooms. Virtual reality (VR) programs allow users to traverse a planet in an imagined galaxy or visit a 3-D replica of a real museum in England. To "enter" these digital spaces, people commonly wear head-mounted visual displays with headphones and hand controllers linked to a computer or mobile device. With the gear, people can not only see these worlds in 3-D but also interact with them.

Virtual reality is most closely associated with computer games, but it is also becoming more common in several other industries. The military uses virtual reality to safely simulate combat situations. In the health industry, doctors at a children's hospital use VR tools to simulate an operation on a baby's heart to practice before the real operation. VR technology can be used to entertain, train, and educate users, and VR developers are tasked with accomplishing these results by creating or re-creating the fully immersive environments in which users can experience, explore, and learn.

A Few Facts

Number of Jobs
About 10,000 US job postings in 2017

Median Pay
$85,040 in 2019

Educational Requirements
Bachelor's degree in computer science or similar field

Personal Qualities
Spatially minded, imaginative, mathematical

Work Settings
In office with virtual reality equipment

Future Job Outlook
According to projected industry growth, higher than average job growth expected

Whether creating a game or an application for industrial use, VR developers love the excitement of building new experiences for people. "Being able to embody a digital version of myself, explore new worlds, create new experiences, and interact with software in a very physical way all sold me on the technology," writes Liv Erickson, senior product manager with Mozilla. "With virtual reality, human-computer interaction is a critical component that has to be considered at every stage of product development."[50]

A Typical Workday

Understanding how users will interact with the product is essential to developing an engaging VR experience. This means thinking about how people will feel, react, and move when they see, hear, or virtually touch something in the VR environment. To understand this, Mike McCready, applied research chair at Lethbridge College in Canada, begins a project by examining the specific gear as well as the requirements of the product. First he determines what type of headset, such as Oculus Go or Samsung Gear VR, and other controllers will be used. Then he will play with other games and applications using that type of headset and gear to see what works well and what does not. He then tackles his assigned product and thinks about details such as how a user's tilt of the head will affect what can be seen and heard. "Storyboarding for VR involves visualizing in a 3D space," McCready says. "Interaction design is quite different than traditional app design. Positional tracking, gaze input and spatial audio cues are some of the different ways users interact with a VR app."[51]

Andrew Marshall is a VR and augmented reality (AR) developer with 219 Design, an engineering consulting firm. Once he has finished with the design stages, much of his time is spent programming. During this step, he often stops and tests his code. Unlike most program testing, VR coding requires physical action during the tests. "Developing for VR is a much more physical experience than making traditional applications," Marshall says.

"Hitting run and watching a command line output doesn't cut it. You need to put on a headset, stand up and walk to the VR space, and wave around your hands with controllers."[52] Using what he sees and feels when testing, he will then modify his program and go through the process again.

Justin Brand is chief executive officer and cofounder of Osso VR, a company that produces hands-on medical device training through VR programs. Throughout the entire development process, Brand says that his company's daily focus is ensuring the virtual medical procedures are realistic. "The biggest challenge by far is getting the 'feel' of the procedures to be as true to life as possible while also maintaining an intuitive and user-friendly experience," he says. "We spend a huge amount of time collecting formal feedback from surgeons of all skill levels to ensure we are developing a product that is both effective and a best-in-class experience that our users love."[53] Generating a good user experience in a digital setting that adequately fools the mind is the goal of VR developers.

Education and Training

There is no set path to working as a VR developer, since it is a relatively new field, but generally companies prefer to see an educational background in computer science and programming. A bachelor's degree in computer science or anything related would be helpful to someone wanting to break into the field. High school students interested in the field would benefit from computer-related classes as well as creative classes like graphic arts.

Although a degree is beneficial, aspiring VR developers can learn on their own through online courses. Unity and Unreal game engines are available to download for free, and they can be used to develop VR programs. On the Unity and Unreal websites, there are user guides, online support, video tutorials, and a forum for troubleshooting. Additionally, these and other companies offer more in-depth VR courses that students can pay to take and that will lead to certification. Motivated individuals can use the many resources online to learn the skills needed for this job and thus increase their chances of getting hired.

Skills and Personality

Imagination is a must for VR developers since they design new worlds or virtual versions of existing ones. Additionally, developers should be good observers—they need to understand how people react, both physically and emotionally, to what they see and hear in order to program a world appropriately. Being detail oriented is also desirable because every detail in the developed worlds is important, since the overall product must feel as real as possible to users.

As for skills, developers need to understand geometry because it is used when creating 3-D objects and determining where to place them in simulated worlds. Programming skills and the ability to learn new programming languages are also a must because VR developers often do the programming themselves.

Working Conditions

Most VR developers work for companies that provide VR products to clients. These developers work in office areas with VR

To get a feel for the user experience, virtual reality developers don headsets and wave their hands or move around. This helps them decide what they need to modify to create an engaging virtual reality experience.

equipment. Developers usually sit to code their projects, but they also stand up and actively test their work using hand controllers and headsets. Testing their products involves moving around and interacting with the product to find bugs, glitches, or anything that would not feel right to a user. The one downside to testing is that it can lead to a commonplace problem. As Marshall explains, "I have a problem that many VR users have: motion sickness. This can especially be a problem when an application is under development."[54]

Despite bouts of motion sickness, developers find the VR field exciting because it involves cutting edge technology and working with others who are equally fascinated by it. Erickson loves her work as a VR developer at Mozilla because of the people she interacts with throughout the day and the combination of technical and creative skills needed to develop her projects. She states, "I get to work with amazingly talented people who have a number of different skills, and I get to constantly be learning about the intersection of writing code for virtual reality, and 3D art. I also love that, because I work on a small team, my role is very dynamic."[55]

Employers and Pay

Major employers of VR developers include companies in the gaming industry, including Oculus VR (now owned by Facebook), Sony, and Nintendo. According to its survey of more than nine hundred developers, Informa Tech, a technology research firm, found that games are still the main generator of jobs in the VR industry, with 59 percent of developers' current projects falling within this entertainment field. However, the survey saw extensive growth in a number of other fields, such as education (33 percent) and training (27 percent). As more industries see the possibilities of VR, the field in general will likely grow.

ZipRecruiter has found that the 2019 average entry-level VR developer salary was $85,040 in the United States, with the majority earning from $60,500 to $106,500 across the United States. Experience is the main factor in determining whether a developer makes more or less than the average.

What Is the Future Outlook for Virtual Reality Developers?

The future is wide open for VR as technology and accessibility advance. The AR/VR market amounted to $16.8 billion in 2019 and is expected to expand to $160 billion by 2023, according to Statista. Per a forecast from International Data Corporation, shipments of AR/VR headsets will rise 67 percent from 2019 to 2023.

One reason the use of VR is predicted to increase is the decreasing cost of VR equipment. In 2019 Facebook cut the cost of Oculus Rift virtual reality goggles to $350, which was $250 below what they cost in previous years. Since more users can afford to

VR Is Innovating Other Industries

"With the ability to develop and share projects in a natural 3D space, VR reduces costs, increases collaboration and the speed of development in industries like architecture, manufacturing, and entertainment. Imagine an architect designing the next high-rise hotel, not from a pad of paper or a computer screen, but in a virtual environment where they can literally stand next to the building and change it as if it was a giant construction of Legos."

—Helen Situ, former VR developer and founder of the tech publication Virtual Reality Pop

Quoted in Disruptor Daily, "The VR Influencer Series Part 5: Helen Situ," March 28, 2018. www.disruptordaily.com.

buy VR hardware now, they will likely increase purchase of associated VR games and apps. But enticing consumers is not the only means of growth for the industry. VR use in the military, in education, and in health care is also driving innovation and sales. As more sectors of the economy embrace VR technology, VR developers will have a chance at a lifelong career.

Find Out More

AR/VR Magazine

www.arvrmagazine.com

This online magazine provides articles on the latest developments in both AR and VR. There are links to VR events, VR games, and VR videos. Reviews of VR gear are also included in the magazine.

Oculus

www.oculus.com

The Oculus website provides information on the company's headsets available for purchase by the public. The site lets people explore the type of games, apps, and movies available to play on Oculus. Additionally, there is a forum section for VR users and developers to discuss issues related to Oculus.

Unity

www.unity3d.com

Unity, a company that sells software game engines, has a website from which visitors can download a free version of its game engine and practice creating VR games and apps. The website provides free tutorials and written guides. Also, there is a community section where people can pose questions and discuss development issues.

Virtual Reality Pop

https://virtualrealitypop.com

Virtual Reality Pop was created as an online publication to provide free access to VR information. On this website are articles from all aspects of virtual reality. It includes the latest industry happenings, newest technologies, and future forecasts.

Source Notes

Increasing Opportunities

1. Bob Grove, "It's Time We Harnessed Big Data for Good," World Economic Forum, October 17, 2019. www.weforum .org.

Cloud Solutions Architect

2. Quoted in Amazon Web Services, "What's It Like to Be a Solutions Architect at AWS ANZ?," YouTube, February 19, 2018. www.youtube.com/watch?v=aOiNTVIANngs.
3. Quoted in Amazon Web Services, "What's It Like to Be a Solutions Architect at AWS ANZ?"
4. New Horizons Computer Learning Centers, "How to Become a Cloud Architect," July 9, 2019. www.newhorizons.com.
5. Quoted in Alison DeNisco Rayome, "How to Become a Cloud Engineer: A Cheat Sheet," TechRepublic, January 28, 2019. www.techrepublic.com.

Computer Vision Engineer

6. Quoted in Manu Jeevan, "Interview with Computer Vision Expert Adrian Rosebrock," Big Data Made Simple, October 12, 2015. https://bigdata-madesimple.com.
7. Quoted in Jennifer Polk, "Transition Q & A: Lino Coria, Computer Vision Engineer," UA/AU, December 12, 2016. www .universityaffairs.ca.
8. Quoted in Jeevan, "Interview with Computer Vision Expert Adrian Rosebrock."
9. Aaron Lazar, "Top Ten Computer Vision Careers You Must Know," Packt, April 5, 2018. https://hub.packtpub.com.
10. Quoted in Olivia Krauth, "The 6 Most In Demand AI Jobs, and How to Get Them," TechRepublic, October 24, 2017. www .techrepublic.com.
11. Zeeshan Zia, "What a Typical Day Is Like Working on Self-Driving Cars," *Forbes*, December 13, 2012. www.forbes. com.

12. Quoted in Jeevan, "Interview with Computer Vision Expert Adrian Rosebrock."

Cybersecurity Analyst

13. Quoted in CityJobs, "A Day in the Life of a Cyber Security Expert," May 25, 2017. www.cityjobs.com.
14. Quoted in CityJobs, "A Day in the Life of a Cyber Security Expert."
15. Quoted in Rutrell Yasin, "A Day in the Life of a Security Analyst," Dark Reading, April 4, 2016. www.darkreading.com.
16. Quoted in Laurence Bradford, "Cybersecurity Needs Women—Here's Why," *Forbes*, October 18, 2018. www.forbes.com.
17. Quoted in Elka Torpey, "Interview with a Cybersecurity Consultant," Bureau of Labor Statistics, January 2018. www.bls.gov.
18. Quoted in Western Governors University, "What Does a Cyber Security Analyst Do?," August 13, 2018. www.wgu.edu.
19. Jeremy Trinka, "Three Ways to Keep Up with Cybersecurity News," Medium, April 30, 2018. https://medium.com.
20. Quoted in CityJobs, "A Day in the Life of a Cyber Security Expert."
21. Quoted in *Business Times* (Singapore), "Full-On War for Cybersecurity Talent as Threats from Hackers Worsen," August 10, 2019. www.businesstimes.com.sg.

Data Scientist

22. Jason Goldman, "Twelve Things I Wish I Had Known as a Data Scientist," Medium, February 21, 2019. https://medium.com.
23. Quoted in Leaders Online, "Start-Up Nation," 2016. www.leadersmag.com.
24. Quoted in Matthew Mayo, "A Day in the Life of a Data Scientist," KDnuggets, November 2011. www.kdnuggets.com.
25. Quoted in Mayo, "A Day in the Life of a Data Scientist."
26. Quoted in Stephanie Robertson, "Meet the Data Scientist Colin Nugteren," SAS, 2019. www.sas.com.

27. Quoted in Stephanie Robertson, "Meet the Data Scientist Daymond Ling," SAS, 2019. www.sas.com.
28. Audrey Throne, "This Is How a Typical Day of a Data Scientist Looks Like," Big Data Made Simple, March 17, 2017. https://bigdata-madesimple.com.

Machine Learning Engineer

29. Rob Matheson, "Autonomous System Improves Environmental Sampling at Sea," Tech Xplore, November 5, 2019. https://techxplore.com.
30. Quoted in Springboard, "Interview with a Machine Learning Engineer," YouTube, November 29, 2018. www.youtube.com/watch?v=rLZGVgqw5u4.
31. Shanif Dhanani, "The Theory Behind Using AI for Long-Term Stock Analysis," Medium, October 4, 2018. https://medium.com.
32. Quoted in Prajakta Hebbar, "A Day in the Life Of: A Machine Learning Engineer Who Wants to Keep the Planet Clean & Green," *Analytics India Magazine*, September 2019. https://analyticsindiamag.com.
33. Quoted in Mae Rice, "How to Become a Machine Learning Engineer: 3 Pros Share Their Insights," Built In, September 5, 2019. https://builtin.com.
34. Quoted in Thumbtack, "Meet Engineer Carolina Galleguillos," August 15, 2017. https://blog.thumbtack.com.
35. Quoted in Alyson Rayome, "How to Become a Machine Learning Engineer," TechRepublic, October 4, 2018. www.techrepublic.com.

Mobile App Developer

36. Quoted in JobShadow, "Interview with an iOS App Developer," 2012. https://jobshadow.com.
37. Quoted in Christa Terry, "How to Become a Mobile Developer—and Why They're So In-Demand," Noodle, October 15, 2019. www.noodle.com.
38. Hussain Fakhruddin, "A Day in the Life of an iPhone Developer," TeksMobile, May 17, 2016. https://teks.co.in.

39. Randle Browning, "How to Build an Impressive Portfolio Site," Skillcrush, October 29, 2018. https://skillcrush.com.
40. Quoted in ITProPortal, "App Development: An Insider's View," September 19, 2013. www.itproportal.com.
41. Fakhruddin, "A Day in the Life of an iPhone Developer."

User Interface Designer

42. Quoted in Eric Bieller, "How to Become a User Interface (UI) Designer: A Step-by-Step Guide," Career Foundry, February 27, 2019. https://careerfoundry.com.
43. Kyle Markell, "On the Days I Wear My UI Cap," Medium, February 1, 2018. https://medium.com.
44. Quoted in Medium, "A Day in the Life of . . . Jenni M (Senior UX/UI Designer)," June 19, 2019. https://medium.com.
45. Quoted in Ben Davis, "A Day in the Life of a User Interface Designer," Econsultancy, February 27, 2017. https://econsultancy.com.
46. Dawid Tomczyk, "Master the Basics of Visual: How to Become a Self-Taught UI/UX Designer," UX Design, May 18, 2019. https://uxdesign.cc.
47. Quoted in Bieller, "How to Become a User Interface (UI) Designer."
48. Tomczyk, "Master the Basics of Visual."
49. Arin Bhowmick, "Designing a Place for Designers," UX Collective, September 13, 2018. https://uxdesign.cc.

Virtual Reality Developer

50. Liv Erickson, interview with the author, October 19, 2019.
51. Quoted in Mark Metry, "The Complete Beginners Guide to VR Development," VU Dream, February 20, 2017. www.vudream.com.
52. Andrew Marshall, "A Developer's Perspective on Virtual and Augmented Reality," 219 Design, September 4, 2018. https://219design.com.
53. Quoted in Reece Armstrong, "Interview with Osso VR: Discussing Virtual Reality & Physician Training," Medical Plastic News, June 19, 2017. https://www.medicalplasticsnews.com.
54. Marshall, "A Developer's Perspective on Virtual and Augmented Reality."
55. Erickson, interview.

Interview with a Cloud Solutions Architect

Travis Webb is a Google cloud solutions architect. He lives in Norfolk, Virginia, and has worked in the information technology industry for over eight years. He answered questions about his career via email.

Q: Why did you become a cloud architect?
A: [Google] Cloud enables individuals and businesses to do things that were not previously possible by bringing a ton of advanced technology together into a single platform and making it available to everyone. It's natural for me to want to help people use a product that I believe in, and it's no surprise that the cloud market is growing amazingly fast. The benefits are immense and obvious, and the product basically sells itself. For me, it represents the perfect combination of software, systems engineering, and business consulting.

Q: Can you describe your typical workday?
A: It's hard to describe a typical workday because the work is very different day-by-day. But if I zoom out a bit, I can describe a typical work-month. In a given month, I might travel to two or three different cities to meet with various customers, learn about their businesses and their current challenges, and help them understand how they can leverage Cloud to achieve their business objectives. I may be visiting other Google offices to meet with my colleagues and collaborate on a draft for a new solution we are working toward publishing and talk about new ideas. In the remaining time, I'm working either at home or in my office, meeting with my colleagues remotely, or focusing on writing a conference talk or solution draft.

Q: How did you get into this career?

A: I've been interested in computers since a young age and convinced my mom to spend $50 on a book on C++ when I was in middle school so that I could learn how to program computers. I initially saw writing small programs as a fun series of puzzles to solve. I was also very entrepreneurial and tried to build small programs or websites that I could develop into businesses. I started ad-supported forum websites, ran a company that hosted game servers, and would fix and build computers for my friends in high school. I did all this for fun. Only in college did I understand more clearly that I could build a career out of these interests.

Q: What do you like most about your job?

A: Every day is different, and it's absolutely true that you have to keep learning. This is much more than a banal platitude—your knowledge acquired from two or three years ago may have helped shape your current understanding but may otherwise not be directly applicable to the problems you're trying to solve today. This includes the college degree. When you're mid-way through your career in technology, the stuff you studied for a few years in your early twenties has very little relevance five or ten years later, assuming you even remember any of it by then. Its main purpose was to point you in the right direction and provide a foundation to build on for future learning. And the challenges of business are always changing as well. Constantly learning new things and solving new problems is very interesting, and results in work that has almost zero monotony.

Q: What do you like least about your job?

A: I can't think of anything I dislike. Any gripes I may have would pertain only to specific situations and not to the job itself.

Q: What changes do you foresee in this career in the future?

A: Everything. Just as I am working on totally different things than I was five years ago, I expect that five years from now I will also be doing different things and solving different problems than I am today. It's the nature of technology that you don't tend to re-solve the same problems over and over. Once a problem is solved, you turn it into a solution that can be used by others, and move to the next problem, and continue to advance the state of the art.

Q: What personal qualities do you find most valuable for this type of work?
A: In this sense, adaptability is very important. A deep interest in solving these kinds of problems is one of the main things I look for when interviewing candidates, for example. If you care about what you're doing, any missing pieces will fall into place over time. The nature of the job is discovering new and better ways to do things, so you usually don't know how to do something before you do it. Your job is not to know things, your job is to figure stuff out. If you think what you're doing is important, you'll do what you need to do in order to be good at it.

Q: What advice do you have for students who might be interested in this career?
A: First, learn the history of your field and understand why things are the way they are. You will not be spoonfed this knowledge in a typical academic program and you will need to seek it out for yourself: buy old industry magazines, read biographies of computing pioneers such as Grace Hopper, Alan Turing, and Bill Gates, read books on business successes as well as failures, and build a more holistic picture of the industry you're entering. Understanding the historical context will allow you to "speak the language" of business and connect with the senior people who are interviewing you in a way that most of your peers will not be able to.

Other Jobs in Information Technology

Application developer
Applications engineer
Augmented reality developer
Chief information officer
Chief technology officer
Cloud consultant
Cloud system engineer
Computer architect
Computer hardware engineer
Computer network specialist
Cybersecurity engineer
Data analyst
Database controller
Data quality manager
Desktop support specialist
DevOps engineer
Front-end developer
Full-stack developer

Help desk administrator
Help desk specialist
Information technology analyst
Java developer
.NET developer
Network administrator
Software architect
Software developer
Software engineer
Software quality assurance
  analyst
Systems designer
User experience designer
Virtual reality designer
Virtual reality engineer
Web administrator
Web developer
Webmaster

Editor's note: The online *Occupational Outlook Handbook* of the US Department of Labor's Bureau of Labor Statistics is an excellent source of information on jobs in hundreds of career fields, including many of those listed here. The *Occupational Outlook Handbook* may be accessed online at www.bls.gov/ooh.

Index

Note: Boldface page numbers
indicate illustrations.

Adobe Mobile App Development, 50
Aircrackng, 26
Alexander, Candy, 24–25
algorithms
described, 16, 30, 38
probability and, 40
Alvarez, Hannah, 52
App Developers Alliance, 51
application backend, described, 44
AR/VR Magazine, 66
AWS Certified Solutions Architect
Professional, 14
Azure Blog, 14

Bartlett, Matt, 54
Bhowmick, Arin, 56
big data, described, 5
Bourke, Daniel, 41
Brand, Justin, 62
Browning, Randle, 46
Brownle, Jason, 43
Bureau of Labor Standards (BLS)
earnings
computer vision engineers, 20
cybersecurity analysts, 27
job outlooks, 4
cybersecurity analysts, 27–28
web developers, 58
Occupational Outlook Handbook,
75
Burtch Works, 35

Callahan, Jeremy, 50
Capital One Financial Corporation,
22
Carnevale, Randy, 33

certifications
cloud solutions architects, 11
cybersecurity analysts, 25
data scientists, 33
machine learning engineers, 40
mobile app developers, 47
user interface designers, 55
cleaning data, described, 32
cloud, the, 4, 8
cloud computing, described, 4–5
cloud solutions architects
basic facts about, 8
earnings, 13
educational requirements, 10–11
employers, 9, 12–13
information sources, 14
job description, 8–10, 12, **12,** 72,
73–74
job outlook, 12, 13–14
personal qualities and skills, 11,
74
Cloud Tweaks, 14
CNNMoney, 50
coding, 46
computer vision engineers
basic facts about, 15
earnings, 20
educational requirements, 18
employers, 20
information sources, 21
job description, 15–18, 19–20
job outlook, 20–21
personal qualities and skills, 18–19
Computer Vision News (magazine),
21
Comyns, Matt, 26
Coria, Lino, 17
Cyber Defense Magazine, 28
cybersecurity, described, 5

cybersecurity analysts
  basic facts about, 22
  earnings, 27
  educational requirements, 24–25
  employers, 26–27
  information sources, 28–29
  job description, 22–24, 26, **27**
  job outlook, 27–28
  personal qualities and skills, 25, 28
Cybersecurity and Infrastructure
  Security Agency, 28
Cybrary, 29

Data Science Association, 36
data scientists
  basic facts about, 30
  earnings, 35
  educational requirements, 32–33
  employers, 35
  information sources, 36
  job description, 30–32, 34–35
  job outlook, 35
  personal qualities and skills, 33–34
Daw, Ellie, 24
Developers Alliance, 51
Dhanani, Shanif, 38, 39
Dhariyal, Bhaskar, 39
Dice.com, 13
Discover Data Science, 36

earnings
  cloud solutions architects, 8, 13
  computer vision engineers, 15, 20
  cybersecurity analysts, 22, 27
  data scientists, 30, 35
  machine learning engineers, 37, 42
  mobile app developers, 44, 49
  user interface designers, 52,
    56–57
  virtual reality developers, 60, 65
educational requirements
  cloud solutions architects, 8,
    10–11
  computer vision engineers, 15, 18
  cybersecurity analysts, 22, 24–25
  data scientists, 30, 32–33

machine learning engineers, 37,
  39–40
mobile app developers, 44, 46–47
user interface designers, 52,
  54–55
virtual reality developers, 60,
  62–63
employers
  cloud solutions architects, 9,
    12–13
  computer vision engineers, 20
  cybersecurity analysts, 26–27
  data scientists, 35
  machine learning engineers, 42
  mobile app developers, 48, 49
  user interface designers, 56
  virtual reality developers, 65
Equifax, 5
Erickson, Liv
  on characteristics of virtual reality
    developers, 63
  on coworkers, 64–65
  on job as virtual reality developer,
    61
Evans Data Corporation, 49

Fakhruddin, Hussain, 45–46, 48
freelancing
  mobile app developers, 48, 49
  user interface designers, 56
Frietzsche, Randall, 25

Galleguillos, Carolina, 41
Galloway, Leigh-Anne, 23, 26
Gartner, 13
Gemalto, 35
Glassdoor, 42, 49, 57
Glen, Stephanie, 34
Goodman, Jason, 31
Good UI, 58
Google AI, 43
Gordeev, Andrey, 50
Grove, Bob, 5
Gurari, Danna, 19
Gurova, Dasha, 16
Guru 99, 43

hacking, 22
Hendley, Imran, 40

Indeed, 20, 35, 42, 49
Informa Tech, 65
information technology (IT) field
  building blocks of, 11
  career possibilities, 75
  number employed in, 4
InfoWorld Cloud Computing, 14
International Data Corporation, 42,
  65

job descriptions
  cloud solutions architects, 8–10,
    12, **12,** 72, 73–74
  computer vision engineers, 15–18,
    19–20
  cybersecurity analysts, 22–24, 26,
    27
  data scientists, 30–32, 34–35
  machine learning engineers,
    37–39, 40–41
  mobile app developers, 44–46, **48,**
    48–49
  user interface designers, 52–54,
    56, **57**
  virtual reality developers, 60–62,
    63–65, **64**
job outlooks, 4
  cloud solutions architects, 8, 12,
    13–14
  computer vision engineers, 15,
    20–21
  cybersecurity analysts, 22, 27–28
  data scientists, 30, 35
  machine learning engineers, 37,
    42–43
  mobile app developers, 44, 49–50
  user interface designers, 52,
    57–58
  virtual reality developers, 60,
    65–66
  web developers, 58
Joyner, Ian, 45, 47
KDnuggets, 32
KeePass, 26
Kleyman, Bill, 11

Lazar, Aaron, 18
Learn UI Design, 58
Ling, Daymond, 33–34
LinkedIn, 13
Linowski, Jakub, 58

machine learning engineers
  basic facts about, 37
  earnings, 42
  educational requirements, 39–40
  employers, 42
  information sources, 43
  job description, 37–39, 40–41
  job outlook, 42–43
  personal qualities and skills, 38,
    40, 41
Machine Learning Mastery (website),
  21, 43
Mahapatra, Chirag, 38–39
Markell, Kyle, 53, 58
Marshall, Andrew, 61–62, 64
Massachusetts Institute of
  Technology (MIT), 37
Matheson, Rob, 27–28
MATLAB, 16
Mauer, Thomas, 13
McCready, Mike, 61
Michelangeli, Marco, 32
Mirza, Shahmeer, 17–18
mobile app developers
  basic facts about, 44
  earnings, 49
  educational requirements, 46–47
  employers, 48, 49
  information sources, 50–51
  job description, 44–46, **48,** 48–
    49
  job outlook, 49–50
  personal qualities and skills, 47
mobile app users, number
  worldwide, 44
Moulden, Steve, 28

National Cybersecurity Center (NCC),
  29
New Horizons Computer Learning
  Centers (website), 11
Nickolaisen, Niel, 47

Nmap, 26
Nugteren, Colin, 33

*Occupational Outlook Handbook
    (BLS),* 75
Oculus, 66
Onward Search, 57–58
OpenCV (website), 18, 21

Password Safe, 26
PayScale, 42, 50
personal qualities and skills
    cloud solutions architects, 8, 11,
        74
    computer vision engineers, 15,
        18–19
    cybersecurity analysts, 22, 25, 28
    data scientists, 30, 33–34
    machine learning engineers, 37,
        38, 40, 41
    mobile app developers, 44, 47
    user interface designers, 52,
        55–56
    virtual reality developers, 60, 63
personal skills. *See* personal qualities
    and skills
providers, cloud services, examples
    of, 8
Purcell, Brandon, 19
PYImage (website), 21
Python, 16

Radinsky, Kira, 31–32
Ramamurthy, Pavi, 24
Rosebrock, Adrian
    as consultant, 17
    on enabling computer to derive
        meaning from images, 15–16
    on job outlook for computer vision
        engineers, 20
    website of, 21

SailGP, 45
Salary.com, 13
Site Inspire, 59
Situ, Helen, 66
solutions engineers, 10, **12**
Speech Therapy for Apraxia app, 45
Statista, 49–50, 65

365 Data Science, 36
Throne, Audrey, 34
Tomczyk, Dawid, 55
Tractica, 20–21
training. *See* educational
    requirements
Treinen, Jim, 23–24
Trinka, Jeremy, 25

Unity, 67
Usability, 59
user interface (UI), described, 44
user interface (UI) designers
    basic facts about, 52
    earnings, 56–57
    educational requirements, 54–55
    employers, 56
    information sources, 58–59
    job description, 52–54, 56, **57**
    job outlook, 57–58
    personal qualities and skills, 55–
        56

virtual reality (VR), described, 60
virtual reality (VR) developers
    basic facts about, 60
    earnings, 65
    educational requirements, 62–63
    employers, 65
    information sources, 66–67
    job description, 60–62, 63–65, **64**
    job outlook, 65–66
    personal qualities and skills, 63
Virtual Reality Pop, 67

Wallenberg, Paul, 13–14
We Are Social, 44
Webb, Travis, 72–74
Weiss, Gregg, 45
Women in Cyber Security, 29
Women in Data Science (WiDS), 36
Women in Machine Learning and
    Data Science (WIMLDS), 43
Woods Hole Oceanographic
    Institution, 37

Zia, Zeeshan, 19
ZipRecruiter, 57, 65

About the Author

Leanne Currie-McGhee has written educational books for over fifteen years. She lives in Norfolk, Virginia, with her husband, Keith, and two daughters, Grace and Hope.